Charleston Public Library
P.O. Box 119
Charleston, ME 04422

D0103430

P9-DDH-095

DAVID BUSHNELL AND HIS TURTLE

THE STORY OF AMERICA'S FIRST SUBMARINE

BY **JUNE SWANSON**

ILLUSTRATED BY **MIKE EAGLE**

Atheneum 1991 New York

Collier Macmillan Canada
Toronto
Maxwell Macmillan International Publishing Group
New York Oxford Singapore Sydney

In memory of Nick DeRita,
my father-in-law and friend
—M. E.

To Stan,
with love and gratitude
—J. S.

Text copyright © 1991 by June Swanson
Illustrations copyright © 1991 by Mike Eagle

All rights reserved. No part of this book may be reproduced or transmitted in any form or by any means, electronic or mechanical, including photocopying, recording, or by any information storage and retrieval system, without permission in writing from the publisher.

Atheneum
Macmillan Publishing Company
866 Third Avenue
New York, NY 10022

Collier Macmillan Canada, Inc.
1200 Eglinton Avenue East
Suite 200
Don Mills, Ontario M3C 3N1

First edition   Printed in the United States of America
1   2   3   4   5   6   7   8   9   10
Library of Congress Cataloging-in-Publication Data
Swanson, June.
David Bushnell and his turtle: the story of America's first submarine / by June Swanson; illustrated by Mike Eagle.—1st ed.
p.   cm.
Includes bibliographical references.
Summary: A biography of the eighteenth-century Connecticut farmer who invented the submarine first used in naval warfare during the American Revolution.
ISBN 0-689-31628-3
1. Bushnell, David, b. 1740—Juvenile literature.   2. Naval architects—United States—Biography—Juvenile literature.   3. United States—History—Revolution, 1775-1783—Naval operations—Submarine—Juvenile literature.   4. United States—History—Revolution, 1775-1783—Naval operations, American—Juvenile literature.   5. Submarine boats—History—Juvenile literature.   6. Mines, Submarine—United States—History—Juvenile literature.   7. Inventor—United States—Biography—Juvenile literature.   8. Bushnell, David. b. 1740.   9. Inventors.   I. Eagle. Michael, ill.   II. Title.
E207.B92S88, 1991
973.3'5'092—dc20   [B]   [92]   90-628

Contents

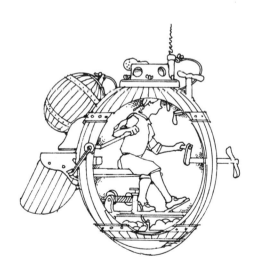

Chapter 1: HOW IT ALL BEGAN

In 1776, men from the thirteen American colonies met in Philadelphia to write a declaration of independence from England. Then came the hard part—fighting for that independence.

Each colony had a small army made up mostly of farmers and storekeepers. They chose a farmer from the Virginia colony as their leader. His name was George Washington.

The colonies needed ships for a navy. Because the thirteen colonies stretched along the Atlantic Ocean (from Massachusetts in the north to Georgia in the south), the sea was important to them. Many men made their living from the ocean. Some were fishermen. Others were traders, boatbuilders, or sailors.

At first, the colonies turned some of their trading ships into fighting ships. Soon, shipbuilders were building real warships as well. During the revolutionary war (called the American War of Independence), fifty-three ships served in the new American navy.

Maybe fifty-four—if you count a funny-looking little boat called the *Turtle*.

Chapter 2: THE FUNNY-LOOKING BOAT

The *Turtle* may have been funny looking, but it was an amazing boat. It was made to travel *under* water. A few inventors in Europe had already tried to build underwater boats. But those boats were all experiments. The *Turtle* was the world's first real working submarine. It was also the first submarine to be used in a war.

The name *Turtle* came from its strange shape. It looked like two turtle shells set on end and glued together.

Another strange thing about the *Turtle* was that it wasn't made by a shipbuilder. It was made by a farmer from Connecticut. His name was David Bushnell. He had never built a boat before. He didn't have a factory or any fancy tools. As a matter of fact, the *Turtle* was built in a shed on a friend's farm.

Many of the ideas David used in the *Turtle* turned out to be very good ones. Many of them are still used (with modern changes, of course) in submarines today.

This is the story of David Bushnell and that first submarine—of their adventures and of their misfortunes.

Chapter 3: YOUNG DAVID

David Bushnell was born on his father's farm near Saybrook, Connecticut, on August 30, 1740. Six years later, his brother, Ezra, was born. Then three girls, Dency, Lydia, and Sarah, were added to the family. Neighbors lived far apart, and there were few children David's age for him to play with. He spent most of his free time alone, reading books.

He loved to read. And he loved to learn. David wanted to know about everything. But work on the farm kept him busy, and there was little time for school.

When David was twenty-seven, that all changed. First, his father died. Then, shortly after, Dency and Lydia died, too. His mother remarried and took young Sarah with her. She left the farm to David and his brother, Ezra.

This was David's big chance. He sold his half of the farm to his brother. At last he had the money—and the time—to go to college.

David knew he first had much to learn. He moved into town and found a teacher to help him—the Reverend John Devotion. Reverend Devotion was the pastor of the local Congregational church and probably the most educated man in Saybrook.

Chapter 4: DAVID AT YALE

After spending two years with Reverend Devotion, David was ready to enter Yale College. This was 1771, five years *before* the Declaration of Independence was signed. But even then, many colonists were complaining about the way England was treating them.

England was forcing them to pay more and more taxes. There were new taxes on tea, glass, paper, and paint. And English soldiers were being sent everywhere to collect the taxes.

The year before David went to Yale, people in Boston proved how angry they were. A group of Boston citizens grabbed sticks and made snowballs to throw at the English soldiers. They shouted, "Let's drive out these rascals."

After a few snowballs were thrown, some of the soldiers shot into the crowd. Three men were killed and eight were wounded. The colonists called it the Boston Massacre.

Talk of war was everywhere the year David Bushnell went to Yale. Maybe that's why he became interested in gunpowder.

Some of his ideas were about how gunpowder could be exploded underwater. Most of the teachers and students didn't think this was possible.

So David began testing. First, he put two ounces of gunpowder into a wooden pipe. He sank the pipe four feet underwater. Only its top stuck out. Then David lit the gunpowder in the top of the pipe...and the whole pipe blew up! He knew he was on the right track.

His next test was much bigger. He put two *pounds* of gunpowder into a wooden bottle. On top of the bottle, he put a two-inch-thick oak plank. Then, on top of the plank, he put a large barrel called a hogshead. The hogshead was loaded with stones. This held the bottle of gunpowder deep in the water.

Again, a wooden pipe ran down through the hogshead and the plank into the bottle at the bottom. The pipe was filled with gunpowder, too. David lighted the top of the pipe. The powder burned all the way to the bottom and the wooden bottle exploded. As David Bushnell wrote, it "produced a very great effect; rending the plank into pieces; demolishing the hogshead; and casting the stones and the ruins of the hogshead, with a body of water, many feet into the air, to the astonishment of the spectators."

David had proved that gunpowder could be fired underwater. Now he wanted to use his findings. He spent much of his time during those college years thinking about this idea. By 1774, he wrote that he was drawing plans for a "sub-marine mine." The next step was to figure out some way to use the mine.

No one knows if David had read about any of the early submarine experiments in Europe. But by his Christmas vacation in 1774, he wrote that he was making plans for a "Sub-Marine Vessel" that would attach his mine to enemy ships.

That spring, in 1775, the War of Independence started. There were battles at Lexington and Concord in Massachusetts.

A few months later, David graduated from Yale. Because of the war, Yale closed two weeks early that summer. A quiet graduation was held in the college library.

Chapter 5: THE *TURTLE* IS BORN

David went back to Saybrook and spent the next two months building the *Turtle*. He worked in a shed at Ayers Point on the Connecticut River. He thought this remote spot would keep his boat secret from the British.

Friends wanted him to ask the government for help, but David chose to build the boat on his own. Several times, he had to stop until he could get more money. By August, the boat was finished. His friends looked forward to the test.

One friend, Benjamin Gale, invited Benjamin Franklin to see this "new machine." Franklin came. After his visit, Gale wrote to a friend in Congress, "Dr. Franklin did me the honor to call upon me, and is now convinced his [Bushnell's] magazine [mine] will contain three times so much powder as is necessary to destroy the largest ship in the [British] navy."

Gale didn't know it, but the local postmaster was a British spy. He opened and copied all of Gale's mail, and then sent the copies to the British governor. So, in spite of all David's work to keep his plans secret, the English found out about the *Turtle*. The governor thought the idea was a joke. He didn't pay any attention to the reports.

But the *Turtle* was no joke. The tests proved that it worked.

The little boat turned out to be about six feet high, three feet wide, and four feet long—just big enough for one man to squeeze inside. It was made of heavy oak planks. The spaces between the planks were sealed with tar to keep the water out. And then iron bands were shaped around it—like the bands around a wooden barrel.

Air came in through two tubes that floated on top of the water. The tubes were fitted with cork valves that closed when they submerged. The *Turtle* could hold about a thirty-minute supply of air.

There was a brass entrance on top of the boat from which the operator let himself in, feet first. Small glass windows in the brass top let light in when the boat was above water. This same idea is still used in modern submarines. Now it's called a conning tower.

On the bottom of the *Turtle* were hundreds of pounds of lead to keep the boat upright in the water.

The driver sat on an oak beam inside the ship. Around him were all sorts of cranks and handles. He almost had to be a juggler to keep everything going.

One crank turned a screw-type propeller that made the submarine move ahead. This was the boat's only power. There was no motor, and batteries had not yet been invented. If the driver cranked as hard and as fast as he could, the *Turtle* would move at the speed of three miles an hour. (That is, if there was no current or tide to work against.)

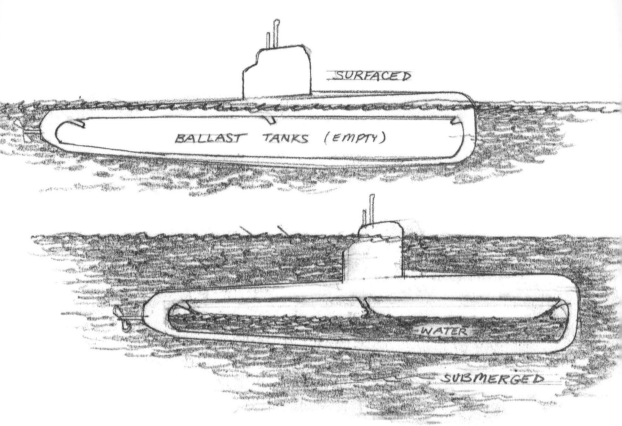

Another crank worked a screw propeller on top of the *Turtle*. This propeller made the ship move up and down once it was underwater.

To steer, the driver had to reach backward and move the rudder behind him. It would have helped if he had three hands!

At the same time, the driver's feet were busy, too. When he wanted to go down deeper into the water, he pushed a foot valve. This let water into a tank at the bottom of the boat, making the boat heavier and helping it sink. Then, when he wanted to come back up, he used two brass hand pumps to pump the water out. Here again, modern submarines follow David Bushnell's model. Today's submarines are controlled by ballast tanks that can be filled with water, causing the submarine to submerge, or emptied, to make it surface.

As if all this cranking and pumping were not enough to keep the operator of the *Turtle* busy, there was also the mine to worry about.

The egg-shaped mine was made from a hollow log. It sat outside the

Turtle, just above the rudder. The mine contained 150 pounds of gunpowder and a "clock" that was set to explode it.

The clock could be set for any time up to twelve hours. When the time ran out, a little hammer stuck a piece of steel, making sparks and lighting the powder. This was the world's first time bomb.

The mine was attached by a rope to a long, pointed wood screw on the top of the *Turtle*. The screw could be turned from inside the boat by one more handle. First, this wood screw was driven into the bottom of an enemy ship. Then, the operator unscrewed a rod inside the *Turtle*, which loosened the bomb from the submarine and left it dangling by the rope from the enemy ship. As soon as the bomb left the *Turtle*, the clock in the bomb started, giving the submarine time to get away.

All this time, the driver's eyes were busy, too. There was a compass to tell him what direction he was going. There was also a gauge that

A.

B.

told him how deep in the water the boat was. Modern submarines have many more gauges, but like the *Turtle*, one of those gauges still tells the water depth.

David thought of everything. He knew it would be dark in the *Turtle* when it was underwater. So he made the water gauge and the tips of the compass of fox fire. Fox fire is a decaying wood that glows in the dark.

But when he tested the boat during the winter of 1775, David found that fox fire froze. And when it was frozen, it didn't glow. He tried using a candle to see in the dark. But the burning candle used up the oxygen in the air too quickly. David's friends wrote to Benjamin Franklin, asking if Franklin knew of something else to use.

While he was waiting for an answer, David showed plans of his boat to the governor of Connecticut and the Council of Safety of

Connecticut (the Connecticut army). The governor and the council approved his work and voted to keep the plans secret. They asked David to continue the tests and said they would repay him for his expenses. David thought he now had a contract with the state. But the agreement was never written down.

Operating the *Turtle* was hard work. David felt he was too frail for it. His brother, Ezra, was young and stronger. So Ezra got the job. All spring and summer, Ezra practiced. He worked hard and became very good at operating the *Turtle*.

The warm weather of spring melted the fox fire. The compass and water gauge glowed in the dark again. David also put in a new pump in place of one that had been causing problems.

Now everything was ready for a test against the enemy.

Chapter 6: WILL IT WORK?

That summer, a large English fleet was blocking New York Harbor. The fleet included ten warships, twenty frigates, and hundreds of smaller troop ships and supply ships. The American captain Samuel Richards reported that there were more than three hundred British ships there. When "they spread their sails to dry—after a rain—" he wrote, "they covered a large extent of water."

With all those ships blocking the harbor, no trading ships could get in to bring goods to the American colonists. No ships could get out to take products for trade to Europe. Fishing ships couldn't even get out into the ocean.

The Americans wanted to drive the English out of the harbor. They thought if the *Turtle* could blow up one of the British ships, it would scare the English into leaving.

David and Ezra moved the *Turtle* to New York. But almost immediately, Ezra came down with typhoid fever. Now he was no longer strong enough to operate the boat.

Quickly, David and the Connecticut officers searched their army for a man who could handle the work. They chose a twenty-seven-year-old sergeant, Ezra Lee of Lyme, Connecticut.

David Bushnell gave Lee a crash course—teaching him about the cranks, the handles, the pumps, and the gauges. Lee had to learn in a few days what Ezra Bushnell had been working on all spring and summer.

Late in August, the English landed fifteen thousand soldiers on Long Island. In a battle that lasted only two and a half hours, the British took the island. When David heard of the defeat, he knew he couldn't wait any longer.

A black, moonless night was chosen for the test. It was September 6. The tide had to be just right, calm and slack.

That night, the English fleet was at anchor just north of Staten

Island. The *Turtle*'s target was to be the flagship of the fleet, a sixty-four-gun warship named the *Eagle*.

At exactly eleven o'clock, the *Turtle* left the dock, towed by two American whaleboats. The boats rowed as near to the English fleet as they dared. They untied the little submarine and silently rowed back to shore.

Lee felt the tide was still too strong. He cranked the *Turtle* around on top of the dark waters for almost two and a half hours. At last, the tide slackened. Now he could come in close under the sixty-four guns of the warship.

Lee shut the door and pushed the foot valve down. The ship sank deeper and deeper under the water. Lee cranked on his propellers until he was under the *Eagle*.

He took the handle of the mine's wood screw. Quickly he began turning. But the screw hit hard metal and wouldn't dig into the bottom

of the boat. Some people said afterward that the *Eagle* had a coat of copper on its bottom, and that the screw wasn't strong enough to bite into the copper.

David Bushnell didn't agree. He thought Lee had hit an iron bar on the rudder hinge. David said it would have been easy for the screw to pierce copper, because copper is a soft metal.

Sergeant Lee knew dawn was coming, but he wanted to make one more try. He moved the *Turtle* along the bottom of the ship, but somehow the ship got away from him. Maybe the tide was coming in and its force pushed him away. At any rate, he couldn't find the ship's bottom again.

By now it was light. The sergeant knew he had to leave. Then, for some reason, his compass didn't work. The only way Lee could tell where he was going was to come up every few minutes and look around.

One of these bobs above water brought him near the British fort on Governor's Island. The guards saw him. Quickly they sent out a twelve-man longboat to check on the funny-looking thing in the water.

When the longboat got within about fifty yards of him, Lee let the mine go. He hoped the men on the boat would pick it up and take it back to the fort. But the English were too smart. They were afraid of a trap and rowed back to the island as fast as they could.

Sergeant Lee made his way to New York. The mine floated into the East River where, Lee reported, it "went off with a tremendous explosion, throwing up bodies of water to an immense height."

The first test of the *Turtle* failed to blow up an English ship, but it did prove some important things. It proved the *Turtle* could safely get under an enemy ship and back out again safely. It proved the clock on the mine worked, giving Lee time to get away. It proved the mine would explode in water.

And it proved that Ezra Lee was a very brave man. David always felt that with a little more training, Lee would have been able to find another place on the ship's bottom to plant the mine that night. And if he had, it might have changed the whole course of the war.

But this bit of bad luck was just the first in a long line of accidents that would haunt David Bushnell.

A few days later, the *Turtle* was given another chance—against an English ship lying off Bloomingdale, at what is now about 106th Street in New York City. This time, Lee tried to tie the bomb just under the waterline. A sailor on the ship saw him and called out an alarm. When Lee dived down to hide, the tide swept him away from the enemy ship. Lee wasn't able to find that ship again, either.

Once more, bad luck had kept the *Turtle* from success.

At the same time, David had been training another operator—an old friend, Phineas Pratt. Pratt had helped him build the clock that went in the time bomb.

Both Pratt and Lee took the *Turtle* out several more times against the British. But one thing after another happened, and they never succeeded in blowing up an enemy ship.

One try was on a cloudy night. Then, just as Pratt was within a few feet of the enemy ship, the moon came out from behind the clouds. Sailors on watch saw the *Turtle*. They called out, "Who's there?"

Pratt and the *Turtle* dived underwater and came up about a half mile away. The enemy ship came after them and even shot at them, but the *Turtle* escaped.

That wasn't the end of the *Turtle*'s bad luck. A few days later, while the *Turtle* was being carried up the Hudson River on a boat, a British warship sank the boat—and the *Turtle*.

Later, David was able to get his submarine out of the river. But he was in poor health and again he was out of money. He also knew he needed to spend more time training his operators. He later wrote to Thomas Jefferson, "I therefore gave over the pursuit for that time, and waited for a more favorable opportunity, which never arrived."

Chapter 7: IF AT FIRST YOU DON'T SUCCEED

Instead of getting the *Turtle* back in working order, David tried other ways to lay his water mines.

In one test, he put out two mines joined by a six-hundred-foot line. The mines were supposed to float down the river and wrap around a British warship. The warship that was the target was towing a captured American schooner. Sailors on both ships saw the line and began to pull it in.

But again, luck wasn't with David. The sailors on the American ship got their mine on board first. The mine exploded. Some sailors were killed and the schooner was set on fire. The men on the British warship quickly dropped their end of the line. The second mine didn't explode, and the warship sailed away safe and sound.

David's next plan was to float a bunch of mines into the British fleet anchored in Philadelphia. Each mine was inside a keg, which is a small barrel. Just after Christmas in 1777, the kegs were put into the river above Philadelphia.

But David's luck hadn't become any better. The mines got caught in ice and didn't reach the city for almost two weeks. By then, because of the growing ice, many of the British ships had left the harbor.

To add to the bad luck, two boys in a small boat picked up the first keg. It exploded and the boys were killed. The explosion alerted the few British ships that were left. Their gunners began shooting at the keg mines floating by.

In the end, the British guns finished off the rest of the kegs, in what was known as the "Battle of the Kegs." Only one British barge was blown up.

But the battle did serve one useful purpose. That winter was the low point of the war for America. George Washington's ragged army was freezing in tents and huts not far away in Valley Forge, Pennsylvania. The writer Frances Hopkinson wrote a funny song about the battle. It gave those cold, hungry soldiers something to laugh about at Valley Forge campfires.

The song's twenty-two verses making fun of the British ended with:

> Such feats did they perform that day
> Upon these wicked kegs, sir.
> That years to come, if they get home,
> They'll make their boast and brag, sir.

And the battle served another purpose. It worried the English. They knew the Americans could explode underwater mines, and they never knew when or where these mines might show up next. It made them very careful. They anchored their ships farther and farther from American ports.

But David Bushnell had given up his one-man underwater war. After the Battle of the Kegs, David decided to return to Yale. Records show he earned a master of arts degree. The records don't say what he studied. But letters written to him—and about him—after this time call him Doctor Bushnell.

All this time, David had kept his work on the mines so quiet that few people knew what he had done. In fact, the next year, when he was captured by a small group of English troops, he was soon freed in trade for English soldiers.

The troops had been hoping to seize American army officers, and when they couldn't find any, they took some ordinary citizens instead. David was one of these citizens. But so secret had been his work, the English didn't realize they had captured the man responsible for all the underwater mines.

After this brush with the English, David decided to join the army. He asked the American governor of Connecticut to write to General Washington and recommend him as an officer. Washington made David a captain in the new Corps of Sappers and Miners. *Sappers* were the soldiers who built forts and dug trenches. *Miners* were the soldiers who put out the land mines.

Six months later, the war was over and soon the army was disbanded. David was given four hundred acres of land and five years pay for his services.

Chapter 8: AFTER THE WAR

After the war, David gave the state of Connecticut a bill for his expenses in building the *Turtle*. New men were in charge of the state. They couldn't find any written contract with David Bushnell. They didn't want to pay him anything, but at last they gave him only a small amount. David was very disappointed.

This was an unhappy time in his life. He later wrote that for the next few years, he was "seized with a severe illness."

His Yale friends tried to help. One paid him a large amount of money for the four hundred acres David had received from the army. Another friend, Abraham Baldwin, was starting a college in Atlanta. (In time, it would become the University of Georgia.) Baldwin offered David a job at the new college.

David went to Georgia. But for some reason, he didn't want to be known as David Bushnell, the inventor. Instead, Baldwin introduced him as Dr. David Bush, a teacher and medical doctor.

During this time, another Yale friend, Joel Barlow, was living in Paris. Barlow had been very interested in the *Turtle* and in David's underwater mines. He had even written a poem about them.

It is also known that Barlow was a friend of Robert Fulton, an American inventor living in Paris. It is thought that Barlow told Fulton stories about the *Turtle* and how it worked.

A few years later, Fulton built a submarine of his own. He called it the *Nautilus*. He used many of David's ideas, but Fulton claimed they were his own and that he was the inventor of the first submarine.

Many people were angry at the claim. They said Fulton wasn't telling the truth—that David Bushnell had built the first submarine. Even Thomas Jefferson spoke out for David Bushnell and his *Turtle*.

Through it all, Dr. Bush kept quiet. He knew that if he told his side of the story, everyone would find out he was really David Bushnell. By now, he was living in Warrenton, Georgia. He had a very happy life there. He was both a teacher at a private school and a medical doctor. He must have felt that keeping his life quiet was more important than being known as the inventor of the first submarine.

David lived in Warrenton until his death at the age of eighty-four. When he died, he left his property to the children of his brother, Ezra. This was the first time the family had heard from him in almost forty years.

Chapter 9: WHAT HAPPENED TO THE *TURTLE*?

What happened to the *Turtle*?

No one knows.

Even in history, the *Turtle* ran into bad luck. Instead of ending up in a museum, where it could be admired and studied, the machine seems to have disappeared.

One of David's keg mines is in the Smithsonian Institution in Washington, D.C. But all that's left of the *Turtle* itself are a few plans and drawings.

In spite of the bad luck and accidents, David's ideas were successful. He proved gunpowder could explode in water. He designed the first time bomb. The screw propellers he invented for the *Turtle* are still used in ships and boats today. Submarines still use his ballast tanks and his conning tower.

And his *Turtle* was a marvelous machine. It did what it was supposed to do. It took a man underwater—under an enemy ship. It carried a mine that could be exploded (even though Lee's mine didn't go off where it was supposed to). And no matter what happened, it always brought the operator back home safely.

George Washington once wrote to Thomas Jefferson about the *Turtle*: "I then thought, and still think," he said, "that it was an effort of genius."

And it was.

DAVID BUSHNELL'S
UNDERWATER MINE AND
DETONATOR

BIBLIOGRAPHY

Beach, Edward L. *The U.S. Navy: 200 Years.* New York: Holt, 1986.

Clark, Joseph J., and Dwight Barnes. *Sea Power and Its History.* New York: Watts, 1966.

Clark, William. *Naval Documents of the American Revolution.* Washington, D.C.: USGPO.

Grant, Marion. *The Infernal Machines of Saybrook's David Bushnell: Patriot Inventor of the American Revolution.* Old Saybrook, Conn.: Bicentennial Committee of Old Saybrook, 1976.

Johnson, Allen, and Dumas Malone, eds. *Dictionary of American Biography.* New York: Scribners, 1958.

Speck, Robert M. "The Connecticut Water Machine Versus the Royal Navy." *American Heritage*, December 1980: 32–38.

Stambler, Irwin. *The Battle for Inner Space, Undersea Warfare, and Weapons.* New York: St. Martin's Press, 1962.

Stevens, William Oliver, and Allan Westcott. *The History of Sea Power.* New York: Doubleday, 1942.

Villiers, Alan John. *Men, Ships, and the Sea.* Washington: National Geographic Society, 1962.

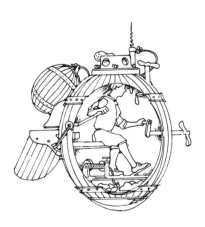

DATE DUE

j973
.3
SWA

Swanson, June
DAVID BUSHNELL AND HIS
TURTLE

Charleston Public Library
P.O. Box 119
Charleston, ME 04422